S0-EGP-399

a Hide-n-Seek Adventure

by Heather Privratsky

illustrated by John Konecny

Published by Orange Hat Publishing 2013

ISBN 978-1-937165-19-2

Copyrighted © 2013 by Heather Privratsky
All Rights Reserved

This publication and all contents within may not be
reproduced or transmitted in any part or in its entirety
without the written permission of the author.

Printed in the United States of America

www.orangehatpublishing.com

My Love—Many thanks to you for your unwavering
support and belief in this book.
To our son and all our children yet to come—I thank
God for the gift of you all.
Zephaniah 3: 17

To Madison,
I hope this book is a
blessing to you & your
family. Enjoy!

Psalm 127

This story is inspired by Psalm 139:

[1] O LORD, you have examined my heart
and know everything about me.
[2] You know when I sit down or stand up.
You know my thoughts even when I'm far away.
[3] You see me when I travel
and when I rest at home.
You know everything I do.
[4] You know what I am going to say
even before I say it, LORD.

[5] You go before me and follow me.
You place your hand of blessing on my head.
[6] Such knowledge is too wonderful for me,
too great for me to understand!
[7] I can never escape from your Spirit!
I can never get away from your presence!

Mama smiled. "I'm sure He would, sweetheart, but no matter where you hide, He will always find you."

"Would He find me under the bed?"

"Oh yes, wherever your little feet tread."

"What about in a great, big tree?"

"Oh yes, even in the tallest hickory."

"Would He find me on a
flying jet plane?"

"Oh yes, even in the clouds and pouring rain."

"Oh yes, He'd find you ever so soon!"

"What if I hid in a long, dark cave?"

"Oh yes, on whatever path you pave."

Mama smiled. "Yes, my dear, it is true what you say.
Instead of hiding from Him, the greatest adventure begins
when you follow Jesus every step of the way."

Dear Jesus,
In the game of hide-n-seek, You will always win.
So, now, I'm ready for the real adventure to begin . . .

CPSIA information can be obtained
at www.ICGtesting.com
Printed in the USA
LVIC070309090513
332947LV00001B

9 781937 165192